Baby Gorillas at the Zoo

Cecelia H. Brannon

Enslow Publishing
101 W. 23rd Street
Suite 240
New York, NY 10011
USA

enslow.com

Published in 2016 by Enslow Publishing, LLC.
101 W. 23rd Street, Suite 240, New York, NY 10011

Library of Congress Cataloging-in-Publication Data

Brannon, Cecelia H., author.
 Baby gorillas at the zoo / Cecelia H. Brannon.
    pages cm. — (All about baby zoo animals)
 Audience: 3+
 Audience: Preschool.
 Includes bibliographical references and index.
 ISBN 978-0-7660-7143-8 (library binding)
 ISBN 978-0-7660-7141-4 (pbk.)
 ISBN 978-0-7660-7142-1 (6-pack)
 1. Gorilla—Infancy—Juvenile literature. 2. Zoo animals—Juvenile literature. I. Title.
 QL737.P94B73 2016
 599.884—dc23
                          2015026953

Printed in the United States of America

To Our Readers: We have done our best to make sure all website addresses in this book were active and appropriate when we went to press. However, the author and the publisher have no control over and assume no liability for the material available on those websites or on any websites they may link to. Any comments or suggestions can be sent by e-mail to customerservice@enslow.com.

Photos Credits: Cover, pp. 1, 3 (center), 6 Edwin Butter/Shutterstock.com; pp. 4–5 Becky Stares/Shutterstock.com; pp. 3 (left), 8 andamanec/Shutterstock.com; pp. 3 (right), 10, 16 Eric Gavaert. Shutterstock.com; p. 12 DavidYoung/Shutterstock.com; p. 14 © iStockphoto.com/mbtaichi; p. 18, Jean-Edouard Rozey/Shutterstock.com; p. 20 Michael Shake/Shutterstock.com; p. 22 Jody./Shutterstock.com.

Contents

Words to Know

| infant | knuckle | troop |

4

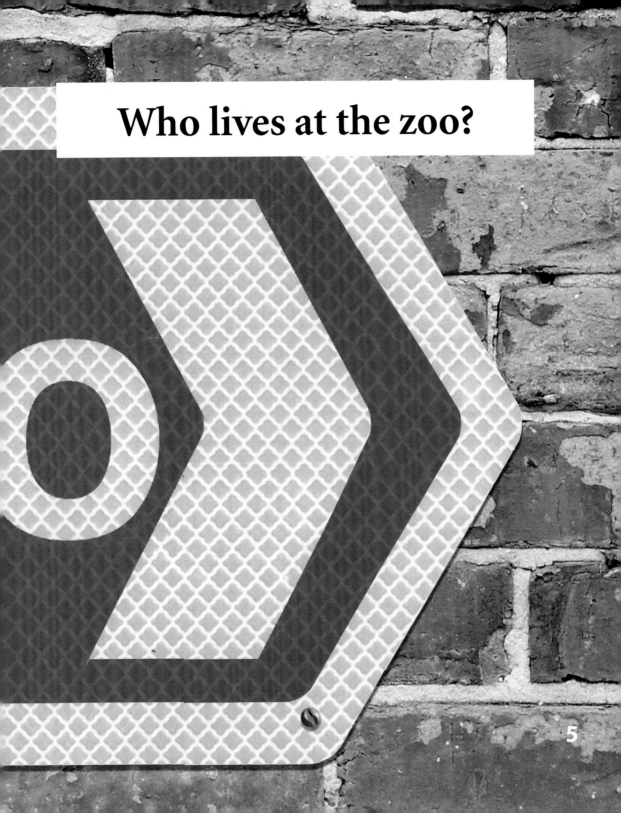

Who lives at the zoo?

A baby gorilla lives at the zoo!

A baby gorilla is called an infant, just like a human baby!

A gorilla infant is covered with black and brown fur. If it is a male, the gorilla will have gray fur on its back when it grows up.

A gorilla infant uses the big toe on its foot like a thumb. It helps the gorilla infant grab food and climb trees.

A gorilla infant rides on its mother's back until it is six months old. Then it uses its legs and the backs of its hands, or knuckles, to walk.

A gorilla infant lives with its family at the zoo. A group of gorillas is called a troop.

A gorilla infant is a plant eater. It eats fruit, vegetables, seeds, and leaves.

A gorilla infant likes to play just like humans do! It has fun playing with toys, chasing other gorillas, and swinging from ropes!

You can see a gorilla infant at the zoo!

Read More

Leaf, Christina. *Baby Gorillas*. Minneapolis, MN: Bellwether Media, 2015.

Saltzmann, Mary Elizabeth. *Baby Gorillas*. San Diego, CA: SandCastle Publishing, 2015.

Websites

San Diego Zoo Kids: Western Lowland Gorilla
    kids.sandiegozoo.org/animals/mammals/western-lowland-gorilla

National Geographic Kids: Mountain Gorilla
    kids.nationalgeographic.com/animals/mountain-gorilla/

Index

Guided Reading Level: D
Guided Reading Leveling System is based on the guidelines recommended by Fountas and Pinnell.

Word Count: 170